CATCHING MURPHY

❖ ❖ ❖

Wilson Ring

The Associated Press
200 Liberty Street
New York, NY 10281
www.ap.org
"Catching Murphy" copyright © 2019
by The Associated Press

Paperback: 978-0-9990359-8-6
(Published by The Associated Press, New York)
E-Book: 978-1-503957-657
(Published byAmazon Original Stories, Seattle)

Cover by Deena Warner Design
Interior design by Kevin Callahan/BNGO Books
Project Oversight: Peter Costanzo
Visit AP Books: www.ap.org/books

*This book is dedicated to the people of
Waterbury who cared about Murphy,
reported his movements, donated to the
Murphy fund and cheered when he was
safely reunited with his family.*

♣ ♣ ♣

*"Catching Murphy" would not have
happened without them.*

CONTENTS

FOREWORD

❖ ❖ ❖

When things go wrong, we come together.

That's an unwritten rule in the small communities of Vermont, where I have long marveled at the creative ways that people find to survive while tested by the forces of nature, lean economies and unruly backyard bears. I saw that in my town of Waterbury when Tropical Storm Irene inundated our downtown in 2011. Residents awoke to four feet of water in their homes, and many were overwhelmed. In their soggy misery, they looked up to see an army of help arriving: their neighbors. Time stopped as we all picked up shovels to save one another. We came through the calamity together.

And so it was that a missing golden retriever triggered that communal reflex. Murphy became an obsession and a passion for a community in central Vermont and beyond. I would hear updates on Murphy sightings at the hardware store and the aisles of the supermarket. Everyone knew—and cared about—Murphy.

Perhaps Murphy is a metaphor for our times. A friend, surviving on the edge of a tumultuous and unforgiving world, needs a helping hand. As the challenge expands, a caring community grows ever larger. In the end, love wins.

In a divided world, a lost dog in Vermont restored people's faith in humanity. Murphy reminded us that there is no problem that we can't solve when we come together.

— David Goodman, journalist,
bestselling author and radio host, Waterbury, Vt.

Murphy in the open field located behind the Ring household, 2014.

1

Encounter

December 2014

✤ ✤ ✤

The town of Waterbury is often described as the crossroads of Vermont. It's here that Interstate 89, which runs from Concord, New Hampshire, through Vermont to the Canadian border, intersects with two-lane Route 100, which takes you north to Stowe or south to the Mad River Valley and the Sugarbush ski resort.

Many of Waterbury's five thousand or so residents live in homes with quick access to the interstate and job centers, yet worry about whether the family cat will become prey to a coyote or fisher. Leave your garbage out or keep the bird feeder up too long in the spring and you'll have bears in your yard; deer can destroy any kind of garden you're trying to tend. But it's a beautiful place to live, among a mix of well-educated professionals and working-class and low-income Vermonters.

Heading north toward Stowe, just past the main Ben & Jerry's ice cream factory, Guptil Road loops around from Route 100 to the heart of Waterbury Center, a triangular New England green complete with a gazebo. The road follows Thatcher Brook, which drains the mountains to the east, and provides access to the homes that climb the side of the mountains.

Since 1876, there's been a farmhouse at the bottom of the valley, still standing on the land that was once the farm that anchored this neighborhood.

That farmhouse was my home.

There's a mobile home park to the west, between the house and Route 100, and a Christmas tree farm to the south, adjacent to our horse pasture. When my wife and I moved here in 1992, the pasture across the brook hadn't been used in decades. We brought it back with brush hogging, thanks to my father-in-law, who owned the local John Deere dealership, and fenced it off to indulge our family lifestyle of keeping horses.

One of the joys of living in the country is being able to look into a field and see wildlife living among the people of the town. It's common to see deer, fox, or woodchucks; through my kitchen window that looks across the brook into the horse pasture, I've also seen mink, otter, and the occasional moose. But one Sunday afternoon in early December, when the grass was brown and patchy with snow, I saw a dog.

A golden retriever was sitting on its haunches just inside the fence that separates our field from the woods beyond. He didn't look scared or lost. I grabbed the binoculars I keep by the back door to get a better look. His red coat looked smooth, and he appeared to be happy and in good health. But he definitely wasn't one of my neighbor's pets that had been allowed to run free.

For weeks, Waterbury Front Porch Forum, the online bulletin board, had carried reports of a dog that ran away after a June car crash in Stowe, not quite ten miles up the road. I just knew this was that dog, but unfortunately he didn't stay long enough for me to do anything about it. The best I could do was go out to the field, put some of our dog's food in a bucket, and place it where I'd seen him sitting.

I rushed back inside to my computer, reported the sighting, and called the phone number included in the postings. A man named Ed Hamel answered the phone immediately, and I breathlessly told him what I had seen. He said he'd be right over—the street address in his postings showed he lived about a quarter mile away. While I waited, I went back to the bucket, only to find the food was gone. I went back to the house, grabbed a leash and more dog food. If Ed would just get here already, I knew we could catch his dog, end of story.

After adding more food to the bucket, I followed the dog tracks—there was more snow in the woods than in the open field, and the tracks were criss-crossed and looked fresh among the hemlock trees, but there were so many I couldn't follow them.

About a half hour passed. Wasn't the guy serious about catching his dog? In the time it was taking him to get here, Murphy could have run miles away. Just as I was starting to get annoyed, an old pickup truck pulled into my driveway. Ed appeared to be in his mid-sixties and was wearing what I would learn was his usual outfit: overalls, with a circuit tester, pliers, and other tools of the electrician's trade sticking out of the pockets. My annoyance disappeared when I learned that he wasn't a neighbor at all. He lived in Morrisville, about half an hour away. He told me he had to use a local address in order to post to Front Porch Forum, which restricts users to their hometowns.

In the previous five months, he'd gotten lots of calls about Murphy and made lots of trips. Hearing that, I wondered if I didn't sound a bit like the boy crying wolf, the latest neighbor promising to bring his dog home. Ed hadn't seen Murphy in almost six months, but he shared stories of chasing down sightings and spells of near-constant calls that would alternate with long stretches of quiet. When called, he went. After all, his family deeply loved and sorely missed their Murphy. And there was a bigger responsibility, which Ed felt keenly: dogs can't live free. When their rabies vaccinations eventually wear off, dogs can pose a threat to other animals and people. Plus, dogs possess no instinctual fear of humans. Escaped dogs are a nuisance more than a danger, eating out of trash cans or chasing barnyard animals. It's not hard to imagine a lost dog being shot by an irate homeowner, especially in rural Vermont, where guns are common.

Ed might have been there an hour that afternoon, roaming the property, looking for his lost pet or any signs of him. At one point, I went back inside and saw Murphy again in my field. Ed was only a couple hundred yards away, in the woods, so I quickly called his cell phone. But Murphy ran off, and Ed never laid eyes on him.

He seemed worn out by his nonstop efforts to find the dog. His voice cracked as he told me how he'd given Murphy up for dead on more than one occasion and how after long stretches without a sighting, he would begin to come to terms with the reality that Murphy was gone. Each new sighting resurrected his hopes, but was tinged with a fear that the three-year-old dog would just disappear ... again, as he had today, perhaps for the last time.

That night, Ed posted to Front Porch Forum, reporting the sighting, its location, and the fact that Murphy had had something to eat. He asked his neighbors to please continue to keep an eye out for his dog.

2

Survival Mode

June 2014

❖ ❖ ❖

That first day I met Ed, he told me the story of how Murphy went missing. More than five months earlier, his twenty-three-year-old granddaughter, Kirstin Campbell — whom he and his wife, Pat, had raised from a young child — was driving the family car one afternoon near the postcard-perfect village of Stowe with Murphy in the back seat. The pair had been tubing with friends on the northern end of the Waterbury Reservoir, which sits behind a dam across Route 100 from my home. It was the first hot summer Sunday, the first time the water was warm enough to swim.

Kirstin and Murphy went tubing two or three times a week. She used a small inflatable boat; Murphy, after all a water dog, would swim along beside her until she'd pull him into the boat and turn him onto his back to rub his wet belly. She was looking forward to what she thought would be another couple months full of days like that one, an idyllic way to pass Vermont's short but glorious summer.

On her way home, Kirstin got a call from one of her friends: "Let's do pizza." She turned off Route 100 and took the back way to the Mountain Road, headed for Piecasso, a local favorite. On either side of the empty road, she saw new corn sprouting in the fields and could smell the freshly cut hay. Classic rock played over the radio. It was a relaxing drive until Kirstin misjudged a slight right-hand curve; her vehicle's wheels drifted off the pavement, and — startled — she overcorrected and lost control. The car crossed the empty oncoming lane, vaulted over a slight bank, and hit a maple tree nearly head-on. The airbag caught Kirstin's head as it slammed forward. She has no recollection of how long she was slumped against the steering wheel. The crash felt like slow motion, but it all happened so fast.

When Kirstin came to, her face hurt. Her nose and lips were bleeding. She checked to see if she had any broken bones. Then she remembered Murphy. She looked in the back seat, and thankfully, he seemed fine. She staggered out of the car, somewhat dazed, and opened the rear door. At first Murphy didn't want to move, but in an instant, he jumped out and bolted, crossing the road back the way they had come and disappearing into a cornfield. It took her a few moments to realize that he was gone. By then the police had arrived, and the officer wouldn't let her chase him. "Murphy, come here, boy!" she yelled into the distance, but it didn't do any good.

✤ ✤ ✤

The police know it's not that unusual for dogs to go missing for a bit after a car crash or a house fire. The trauma sends them into survival mode, an instinct to flee. After their panic subsides, though, they usually come home, or allow themselves to be caught. There was no reason to think that Murphy's adventure wouldn't end the way most lost-dog stories do. Whether it takes a few hours or maybe until the next day, dogs are usually thrilled to reunite with their masters, to return to the nourishment of regular feedings and affectionate human attention.

Still, there is a science to catching lost dogs that have escaped after a traumatic event. The key is to be as nonthreatening as possible. The number-one rule: don't chase them or call them by name. Running after a dog screaming will only increase the animal's fight-or-flight response. Instead, the experts urge patience. A searcher, when spotting a missing canine, should sit or even lie down, not looking at the dog. Some trainers even suggest singing. The dog will investigate and, in most cases, allow itself to be caught.

In the immediate aftermath of her accident, Kirstin and her grandparents were otherwise occupied: Most of her injuries were bumps and bruises, but she spent the night in the hospital to be sure her body wasn't hiding some greater injury. Coping with a family member's traumatic episode, and beginning to cope with the loss of the family car, kept them from the search. Some of Kirstin's friends, however, had arrived on the scene within minutes of the crash, and they immediately headed up the hill, calling Murphy's name, apparently unaware that their calling and chasing was only making it worse. Stuck at the hospital, Kirstin sought help in finding Murphy. She texted and called nearly everyone she knew or could count on, and they scoured the nearby fields, searching up and down the Vermont hills for a dog that, even before the crash, was shy of strangers. At one point, one of Kirstin's friends got within ten or fifteen feet of him, a standoff that ended when Murphy bounded away. Perhaps, they feared, Murphy was lost.

✤ ✤ ✤

That next day was a Monday, and Ed had to work a full shift. He spent much of his time wiring the homes, businesses, and resorts of Stowe, the iconic Vermont tourist town, and the job kept Ed from rejoining the search until early evening, when he began driving up and down the hills near the crash site.

He started by looking near where Murphy went missing. He nurtured a wounded annoyance that Kirstin had crashed the family car and lost her dog, her companion, and here they all were trying to catch him. Ed figured someone would find him sooner or later. But he worried, too, imagining Murphy hit by a car, or getting shot for being somewhere he didn't belong, or simply disappearing forever. He kept on looking, driving, scanning the edges of the field with the skill of a lifelong deer hunter. But rather than the brown coat of a deer, Ed looked for the distinctive rust-colored coat of the dog that Kirstin, two of her friends, and her grandmother had brought home as a four-month-old puppy. Ed called for him, hoping the dog would respond to his familiar voice and come running. But the hours passed, and there was no answer.

✦ ✦ ✦

While she recovered from her physical injuries and her family began to figure out the practical challenge of replacing the car, Kirstin began to beat herself up. "It's like I killed my dog," she told a close friend at the time — the friend who had been with her when she brought Murphy home as a puppy. Despite many reassurances that it was only a matter of time until he was caught, the guilt wouldn't go away. Murphy was more to her than just a pet. He was a loving presence that had helped her weather one of the most traumatic episodes in her own life: About two weeks after she brought Murphy home from the breeder along the Canadian border, Kirstin's best friend committed suicide. Murphy's unbridled exuberance and countless kisses helped carry Kirstin through. She took him everywhere, and she avoided friends who didn't want Murphy at their homes. He never had accidents; she never had to yell at him. "He knew that I needed him," Kirstin said.

So, in those early days, when the slow cruising along the roads of Stowe ended in vain, the family took up the search the old-fashioned way, posting flyers around town on telephone poles and community bulletin boards. They brought their efforts to social media, posting pleas for information on the Stowe "Lost Pet" Facebook page. It was there that Kirstin began to bare her soul to the world:

> *I got Murph 3 years ago, I didn't know it then but he was going to save me. A week later my best friend died. Murph held together what was left, he was with me all the time, he smiled when I couldn't and he hugged me when I didn't want anyone else to see my pain. He's more than a dog, more than a pet to me. He's my rock . . . my everything.*

✦ ✦ ✦

Murphy eluded capture, but he didn't disappear. Sightings were constant but fleeting, will-o'-the-wisp encounters of an animal removing itself from human activity as effectively as any deer or bear in the area.

A day after the crash, a dog fitting Murphy's description was seen digging in the trash at Willie's Village Auto, only a few hundred yards from where the accident occurred. Over the next few weeks, various reports tracked him to a series of nearby mountain-biking trails heading toward Morrisville, a route that, if continued, could have taken him home. He was also spotted just to the south of the crash site in Stowe's Cady Hill Forest, a heavily wooded area crisscrossed by recreation trails. Murphy sightings became fixtures of the "Lost Pet" Facebook page: behind the Golden Eagle Resort, near roads called Gilcrist and Stagecoach and Sterling Valley, by Paine's Christmas Tree Farm. No matter where he was sighted, he wouldn't approach anyone and continued to run whenever called by his name. The Stowe Reporter, a weekly newspaper, ran a story headlined, "Lost and seen, but not yet found."

Experts say that sometimes when dogs go missing they will stay near where they became lost. Other times they'll move. Where they go usually depends on sources of food, or places to hide, or both. About a month after the crash, Murphy took a trip. It's not clear why. It could have been the series of violent thunderstorms that shook the area that summer, the explosions and flashes of light driving him south. It's likely he followed the Stowe Hollow Road out of the village, first uphill, and then down into Waterbury Center, in a straight line, just under ten miles from the crash site. After several weeks of silence, a Front Porch Forum post revived hope:

> *There has been a Irish Setter roaming around our home this week. He's been here 3 times. Does anyone own this beautiful dog and do they know he's roaming? We are so*

close to RT 100 I'm afraid he's going to get
hit by a car. My husband tried to catch him
to see if he had a collar/tags on but he took
off. He seems like a really sweet dog.
—N. Karcher, August 4

Kirstin and Ed didn't understand what had prompted Murphy to roam so far, but the giant paw prints in a compost pile behind the Karcher home plus a ghostly image from a trail camera convinced them it was him. Kirstin had been hoping that he would find his way home—but Waterbury Center was in the other direction from Morrisville. Was the dog confused, or was something that had once bonded him to Kirstin and her family now broken?

3

Sightings

September 2014

✣ ✣ ✣

The mobile home park that abuts my property is
bookended by a narrow copse of hemlock trees and a
number of traditional homes. Several of the mobile
homes were abandoned long ago and have empty
sheds that could offer shelter to a skittish dog. Just
to the south, the Murray Hill Christmas Tree Farm
also provides lots of cover beneath the low-hanging
boughs of the trees. All the trash from nearby homeowners would have given Murphy an occasional
taste of half-eaten pizza, steak gristle, and whatever else folks had discarded from dinner the night
before. The garbage and hiding places combined to
make the perfect setting for a dog that didn't want
to be captured. Indirectly, we were still feeding him.
Murph kept testing the boundaries by making brief
appearances before quickly disappearing again.

The community began pulling together in hopes of bringing him home.

> *I saw Murphy the lost dog on the eastern side of Route 100 Tuesday, 9:35pm, in the area of Lake Champlain Chocolates. I'm sure it was him. It was dark and he was just standing there watching the cars go by . . .*
> — K. Carter, on the Stowe "Lost Pet" Facebook page, August 6

> *Murphy is in Waterbury Center, there was two sightings yesterday (8/5/14). His human misses him and wants him back home.*
> — N. Karcher, Front Porch Forum, August 6.

> *Good News! Today, he was seen in the trailer park off on East Wind Drive, across from the Cabot Cheese outlet on RT 100. If anyone sees him, please don't chase him.*
> — N. Karcher, Front Porch Forum, August 19

Over those first few weeks, Ed, Kirstin, and Pat spent hours looking along East Wind Drive and walking among the Christmas trees, looking for clues. But the routines of life returned before Murphy did, and Kirstin went back to her job at a Stowe restaurant. Ed picked up more of the daily effort to search for Murphy in Kirstin's absence. Pat was supportive and optimistic. They didn't know it at the time, but they were settling in for the long haul. While Kirstin wasn't making the trip to Waterbury herself as much as she had after Murphy was first spotted there, she was still following along, reading the Front Porch Forum and Facebook posts and Ed's daily emails to an ever-expanding group of people.

Everyone knew Murphy was living among the Christmas trees or in the trailers. Many nights, Ed and Pat would buy a pizza from Jimmz, the local alternative to Piecasso, and set up lawn chairs at the Murray farm, hoping their familiar scent and unthreatening appearance would prompt him to walk up to them and ask to be taken home.

It didn't.

✤ ✤ ✤

At wit's end, as the furtive sightings on motion-activated trail cameras that captured ghostlike images of Murphy in the middle of the night piled up, joining reports of sightings behind area homes, Ed borrowed a trap. Where would he set it? He decided to crowdsource the plan.

Lisa Lovelette, a retired elementary school principal and pet sitter who lives in Waterbury Center, saw Ed's posts on Front Porch Forum. Lisa, who has two dogs of her own, was consumed with empathy when she learned how far away Ed lived from Waterbury, and she offered to help with his new plan to trap Murphy. She borrowed another trap from the Central Vermont Humane Society, which lent it to her for five days on the promise that she'd return the trap immediately if the society needed it. Ed and

Lisa set one trap in the woods, the other near Jimmz Pizza. Lisa volunteered to check the traps daily, since she lived nearby. She also made larger flyers and took them door to door in the neighborhood.

They baited the traps with irresistible treats for a dog: rotisserie chicken and bacon. They also put in some of his toys, hoping the familiar scent would snap him out of his wary, wandering posture. The traps caught two cats, a skunk, and at least one dog that belonged to the neighbors. But no Murphy. Though the neighbors were sympathetic to the search and wanted to help, they got annoyed when their own pets were entrapped. Eventually, they asked the Hamels to take the traps away.

In his mounting desperation, Ed found a pet psychic on the internet and decided to give her a try. In her vision, she saw Murphy on a parallel road to one where they had sought him. It was a close-enough description of where Murphy was known to be roaming that they went with it. A lead was a lead. However, spending big dollars on a psychic only to arrive at the same emptiness made Ed feel disgusted, and he and Pat soon gave it up. It's possible, even likely, that Murphy, unable to surrender the self-preservation mode that was keeping him alive, watched them from afar.

By the end of September, the air had turned cold. Rather than having to continually return borrowed traps, Ed built his own. He found a design online from The Retrievers, a Minnesota-based organization that designed a trap for a dog who wouldn't go into a smaller one. The rectangular trap, made of light lumber and heavy wire garden fencing, was bigger and less confining than the metal traps he'd been using. Ed first set it up among the trees at the Christmas tree farm, and then on the property just south of there, where another family had been capturing images of Murphy on the motion-activated trail camera behind their house. After a few weeks, though, the only dog in the trap belonged to the homeowners, and Ed was, again, asked to take it away. A little embarrassed and sad, he put it into the back of his truck.

All the while the reports kept coming from places where Ed was not, which might as well have been everywhere. Regardless, when Ed got a credible report, he would just go, no matter how long of a drive or how much gas it guzzled. He did so with the vision of bringing Murphy home for the holidays, which would be the best present of all to Kirstin. His public commitment was unyielding and inspiring to the many other people who continued to keep eyes peeled for Murphy, but with winter coming, Ed was getting very, very worried.

✦ ✦ ✦

After the first flurries of winter fell on November 15, Ed posted a plea on Front Porch Forum:

> *With snow on the ground please look for tracks coming and going from any barns, sheds or other buildings. He has to be nesting somewhere.*

Then came the third Thursday of November, along with another post from Ed:

Happy Thanksgiving to all Murphy is still out there we hope please keep an eye out for him or his tracks he must be staying in someone's barn or shed or whatever Thanks Ed.

A pall hung over the holidays that year. Kirstin, Ed, and Pat went about the festivities of the season, but they missed their pet and knew he was in the wild, cold, and on his own. They kept hoping for a call that Murphy had been found, while at the same time dreading the news that he was dead. Even worse, they feared that the sightings would stop altogether, leaving Murphy's disappearance an unsolved mystery.

4

Sensation

December 2014

✤ ✤ ✤

I've spent my adult life working as a reporter, so as soon as I heard of the Murphy saga that was unfolding around my home, I knew that he was a story: a beautiful golden retriever lost in the same neighborhood for months, a not-so-scary phantom winning the hearts of a community that was collectively pulling for his return to his family. But for the first time in my career, I was part of the story; applying the same journalistic standards to the lost-dog story as any other matter of municipal concern meant that I could not be the one to tell it. In mid-December, as winter 2014 tightened around us, I passed the missing Murphy story to a coworker, and it played across the world, in syndication, beneath the headline "Bacon, pet psychic turn up zilch in search for dog."

Ed and I hadn't made many formal plans for the

future that first afternoon we met, beyond that I would keep adding food to the bucket to see if we could keep Murphy coming back, and he would come set up his homemade trap. I went out every morning and night to feed and water our horses anyway, so it wasn't hard to add Murphy to my routine, wading the brook morning and night, sometimes accompanied by my yellow lab, Gilly, or our Jack Russell terrier, Mabel, to visit the field shrouding Murphy. Like our own dogs and horses, whose personalities I had come to know and understand, I started to learn the habits, moods, fears, and joys of the dog I'd only seen and never touched.

It was important to me to let Murphy know he could always find food in my field. And I was trying to get him to find it on my terms. Each time I added food to the bucket, I moved it away from the edge of the field where I'd first spotted him, twenty or thirty feet closer to my house. The plans weren't well thought out, but the goal was to get him eating among our human-made horse jumps, then eventually lure him into Ed's homemade trap.

Every day, no matter the location of the bucket, the food would be gone. Murphy was coming to depend on me, and that was good. It never occurred to me that another animal could have been eating the dog food, and as far as I know, in those early days none did. It took about a week to move the bucket across the field to our horse jumps.

A week after my first Murphy sighting, while I was waiting for Ed to arrive with his trap, I again spotted the dog out my kitchen window, again in my field.

While skittish, Murphy looked healthy and like he was having fun, almost frolicking, going where he wanted and eating what he could find. I called Ed right away, and Murphy was still in the field when Ed arrived. Ed went around the corner of my house and called his name. Murphy stopped and looked at the sound. There seemed to be a hint of recognition, but rather than approach the man who had sheltered and fed him since he was a puppy, Murphy took off at a dead run. It was the first time Ed had seen him since before the crash.

He called Pat: "You won't believe it, I just saw Murphy."

Even though I didn't know Ed well, I picked up the stress he was feeling, and I could see what a small victory it was to lay eyes on the dog he'd been seeking those many months.

We hauled his trap across the brook and placed it among the horse jumps. It was designed to be triggered with bait tied to a string that, when tugged upon, would pull the pin in the vertically hung door, which would then fall straight down. But we had no intention of setting the trap right away. Our first goal was to make Murphy comfortable around it and teach him that the trap was a place where he could always find food.

As much as the Hamels wanted Murphy home for Christmas, we just weren't ready to set the trap before the holiday. We didn't yet feel he was comfortable enough around it and didn't want to risk scaring him off. I continued to use the same food bucket that Murphy had followed across the field, moving it ever closer to the opening of the trap and then, finally, just inside the trap itself. After a few days of that, I set the bucket outside the trap but put the food itself on the floor inside. Over the first few weeks, the food kept disappearing. I would replace it, morning and night, and while most of it would be gone, anything put far enough inside to catch him would stay frozen in place at the back.

Murphy was becoming a challenge that I was determined to solve, and I was getting the sense that we needed more tools to do so. In early January, Ed brought a motion-activated infrared trail camera, and we mounted it on a horse jump. Every day, I'd swap the memory card and study the images that had been captured. The photos were in color during the day, but they'd turn a ghostly black and white after dark. They included a time stamp and the temperature. Many images were out of focus, and in some Murphy was barely visible, out of range of the camera's night vision. Other times he would stand for perfect portraits. In one of them, it was clear that he'd somehow removed his collar. The infrared flash would turn his eyes silver, a black-and-white equivalent of red-eye.

These images, and the food that stayed uneaten in the back of the trap, made it obvious that Murphy still didn't trust our human constructs. He was watching from the woods, waiting for me to come out of the house, feed the horses, and then feed him. The tracks in the snow revealed that he used the same route to and from his food, out of the trees between my property and the trailer park. On one occasion, I even saw him from my kitchen as he crossed the field. He sat and stared at the trap, tongue hanging out, panting, a sure sign of anxiety. He'd get up, walk a few feet closer, and then sit again, checking to make sure it was safe to keep going. When he finally arrived, he put his head and shoulders down and darted around some plastic barrels we were using to try to channel him toward the trap's opening. The first few visits after we put his food inside the trap, Murphy would circle it, staring but not daring to go in. More than once, he picked the bucket up with his mouth and pulled it a safe distance from the trap where he would eat in peace. We kept hoping that his need for food would continue to overpower his fear, and it seemed that we were right, at least so far.

"That first step into the trap is always the toughest for them, and after they do it once, they will go back for food," Greg James, of The Retrievers, told us. Greg had sent the message to Lisa, who shared it with the rest of the expanding Murphy crew.

Greg was right. Finally, four days after we set up the camera, Murphy started going into the trap. I kept moving the food just a tiny bit farther inside each time. First it was just his head that needed to enter the trap to get the food, then his front feet. After that, he was going all the way in, although you could still see his anxiety in the photos. Sometimes he'd stretch to reach the food while keeping his back outside. Over time, Murphy relaxed a bit, and it started to look like we may have changed his mind, convinced him that this wasn't a trap, but a trough.

Still, as winter deepened, I worried that Murphy was no longer enjoying himself, that his playful nature had been replaced by a grim determination to survive. We settled into a watchful winter routine, with Murphy at the center: Ed would go to work and then home, always ready to hop in his truck if there was news, or to bring food for Murphy or batteries for the camera. We got support from an ever-expanding group of volunteers who'd bring dog food or ideas, and we stayed in touch with all of them via daily emails, which Kirstin read faithfully. For me, feeding and checking on Murphy was how I began and ended my day. It never occurred to me to quit the search. He became a presence in my life as much as our horses, and my efforts to bring him home gave me an additional sense of purpose.

Photo Gallery:

The Trap

❖ ❖ ❖

A wary Murphy stares at food in the trap that was designed to safely capture him, January, 9, 2015.

Murphy visits the trap during springtime, but is too wary to go inside it, April 29, 2015.

A shaggy Murphy kept visiting and sniffing around the trap throughout the year, June 13, 2015.

By fall, Murphy had lost weight, so the trap was used to keep the hungry dog close by, October 30, 2015.

5

Front Porch

January 2015

✤ ✤ ✤

Murphy's story continued to spread. Every few days, Ed would post a message on Front Porch Forum. The Stowe Reporter and Waterbury Record continued to run periodic stories. The search became more and more of a community quest each day.

Murphy, locked in survival mode, was developing a route that led to sightings on Blush Hill, about two miles south of my field. That scared me: It meant Murphy was crossing Route 100 regularly, probably several times a day. This was a very busy stretch of highway, and I dreaded that our quest to catch Murphy could end by the side of the road.

Many well-intentioned people wanted to help, and we were very grateful for the continued sightings, but it became necessary to guide these efforts to lend a hand. On January 28, Lisa made this plea on Front Porch Forum:

> *We want to respectfully remind folks*
> *to please refrain from feeding Murphy*
> *because we need him to be hungry enough*
> *to enter the trap for his food. If the trap*
> *is his primary food source we have a*
> *much greater likelihood that it will serve*
> *its purpose.*

Lisa also had the foresight to set up an account at a local bank to help Ed and his family pay for what we expected would be significant veterinary expenses after Murphy was caught. The fund started to bring in donations — mostly small ones, but it gave people a way to help.

Meanwhile, Ed and I kept at it. And as the cold continued, I felt more worried every day. So in early January, when I received an offer of help from Peggy Struhsacker, a wildlife researcher who tracks and traps wolves in the western United States (and whom I knew through my work), I was thrilled. She and her husband tracked Murphy through the woods near my field, and Peggy cut hemlock boughs and wove them into the side of the trap, hoping to make it seem more like the nests we knew he was using in the woods. She also put a cooler in our garage loaded with a twenty-pound prime rib that had been slated for disposal by a Stowe supermarket. She let me know via email how to feed it to Murphy:

> *I cut up a lot of chunks and put about five*
> *pieces in the trap and a can of mackerel*
> *cat food . . . I would not put out more than*
> *5 to six chunks of meat — really rich — but is*
> *what he needs . . . He has survived so far so*
> *maybe, like all wildlife in this weather, he's*
> *curled up somewhere.*

The forecast that week called for brutally cold temperatures, pushing thirty below before windchill. It would be the coldest night since Murphy had gone missing. We were all very worried — the entire town was worried. Front Porch Forum had created a winter contest called "FPF's 7 Words for 2015" that drew 1,700 entries statewide. A handful of winners were chosen randomly. Three entries were about Murphy.

Barbara Farr wrote:

> *We want Murphy reunited with his family.*

Alexia Venafra exclaimed:

> *Hoping Murphy the Dog gets home soon!*

Shari Potter spoke for many with this post:

> *I pray that Murphy stays warm tonight!*

The next day, rather than putting Peggy's prime rib inside the trap where Murphy would have to work to get it, I put it near the entrance, lots of it. I wanted to make sure he had enough to eat — enough energy to survive the cold — and didn't see the need to make it difficult for him to get it. An image of a blurred Murphy on the camera just after sunup one morning showed a temperature of negative thirty-three degrees. The food was gone, but so was he.

I put out more food the next night, but the next morning it was still there. It scared me.

So, I sent Peggy an email:

I'm a bit worried. He hasn't eaten what I left him this morning.

She replied moments later:

The food is rich — he might be digesting.

She was right. After skipping one night, Murphy was back, resuming his normal routine.

On Saturday, January 10, in the middle of the day, I watched from my kitchen as Murphy walked up to the trap. I took some photos and showed them to Ed. Murphy appeared comfortable with the trap; he'd go inside it to eat, and he showed up during the day. We decided it was time to set the trap, and we did so the next day. I was nervous but hopeful that we'd be sending Murphy home. I was so confident he'd return on Sunday that at midday I set up a video camera in my kitchen, zoomed in on the trap. I kept glancing out the window, ready to hit "Record."

Nothing.

Discouraged, I turned off the video and unset the trap. But photos I looked at the next day revealed that he had been by two times that evening. And just when I thought I had figured out the pattern of his behavior!

It was then that I decided to reach out to Erika Holm, then president of the board of the Central Vermont Humane Society and the animal control officer in neighboring Middlesex. She'd been following the Murphy saga through my Facebook posts and was thrilled to be asked to help. Erika is a dogcatcher in the best sense of the word. She knows the science of catching lost dogs, and over time she consulted some of the top experts in the field about how to catch Murphy. The bottom line of what the experts said: keep doing what we were doing. In addition to her expertise, she started bringing equipment we'd use to help catch him, including a bright handheld spotlight that could illuminate the trap from my back door.

It was also around then that Ed told Murphy's story at The Old Fishing Hole, a hunting, fishing, and trapping supply store in Morrisville, where a part-time employee named Eroc agreed to check on our trap. He adjusted the tension on the trigger plate and added a scuba-diving weight to the door so it would be heavier and fall faster. Ingenious — and sure to make the trap work properly now. Eroc, a long-time coyote trapper, said, "I see no reason we can't catch Murphy within a week."

We began to wonder what Murphy would be

like if I managed to catch him. Would he be vicious enough that we'd need a long pole with a noose on one end, the type used by animal control, to force him into a kennel? A catch-pole, as they're called, was ready in my garage. Or would he break his defiance and be happy to see me, grateful that at long last we were saving him from himself so he could go home and sleep in front of the Hamels' wood stove? At one point, there was a fierce, almost nasty debate among our small group of animal lovers, all experts in their own field, about which outcome to expect. Peggy, the wolf tracker, even suggested a near-feral Murphy could live out his life in a Minnesota wildlife science center.

But Erika, whose specialty was catching lost dogs and who had done it scores of times, said he'd most likely be fine as soon as he switched out of the survival mode that had kept him alive. For his part, Ed was ready to take Murphy to a vet as soon as he was caught, ready to learn what, if anything, Murphy would need to go through to become a pet again. I told them I didn't care either way. All I wanted was Murphy out of the wild.

I kept the trap set. We were so confident we'd catch him that we kept track of everyone's schedule so that when the moment occurred, we could all get to my field as quickly as possible. During the day when I was working, Lisa would drive over every couple hours to see if we'd caught him. We even had the local vet on standby so she could give Murphy a quick physical before sending him home.

But it was all for naught. Sure, the trap would get triggered overnight — maybe by Murphy, maybe by the strong winds — and sometimes the bait was gone. But Murphy wasn't inside. The nighttime images showed him just standing outside it, staring at the food through the wire mesh. We felt puzzle and duped. Where was our happy ending?

6

The Cold

Thank you so much for the update on Murphy. When I hadn't heard anything for a while, my heart sank. But every night I look up at the stars and pray he is still looking up at them too.

— C. McNair, Front Porch Forum

February 2015

❧ ❧ ❧

With enough to eat, animals can survive the extreme cold, and dogs pass the time when they're not eating curled up with their noses in their tails, saving energy and generating heat. But merely surviving takes everything they have. Photos through the harsh winter showed Murphy with his head down, his brow almost furrowed, hunched and gaunt.

Murphy was walking long loops south from my place to Blush Hill. There were sightings near the dumpster of a Chinese restaurant, near the construction site of a new hotel and an adjacent apartment complex. But those movements meant that he was once again crossing Route 100, putting himself in mortal danger. We'd get reports of him sitting by the side of the road, as though waiting to cross. Other times people would report that Murphy had crossed in front of their car. Every time I'd hear of him near the highway, I cringed.

We talked about sedating him by putting drugs into his food, or shooting him with a dart gun. The former would take about forty-five minutes to bring him down, the latter maybe half as long, but he could still cover a lot of ground in the twenty minutes or so that the dart would need to take effect. Then there was the challenge of getting close enough to him to actually hit him with that kind of projectile while keeping the liquid sedative from freezing. And while Murphy was fine sleeping outside in the cold when well fed, we didn't know how he'd react to a sedative that could slow his metabolism. We worried he might quickly freeze to death.

✦ ✦ ✦

One evening after switching the card in the camera, I was surprised to find a Vermont game warden examining our trap. I would learn his name was Chad Barrett, and after I tracked him down, he told me he'd received a complaint that Murphy was chasing deer. Dogs that chase deer can weaken them to the point where they can't survive the cold. In such situations, wardens first encourage the owner to keep their dogs at home and then fine them if they don't comply. It's rare, but in extreme cases wardens will even shoot a dog to protect the deer.

Chad told me he had crisscrossed the area and, thankfully, found no evidence that Murphy was chasing deer. While he clearly wanted to see Murph returned home — and caught safely — he also told me the law prohibited him from getting involved with domestic animal cases unless he determined that they were causing problems for the area's game.

It wasn't the only bullet that Murphy had to dodge. One day, a very upset Ed called to tell me that a dogcatcher named Peter had accused him of animal abuse and was threatening to shoot his dog on sight. Ed told the whole town the story on Front Porch Forum:

> *Apparently there are persons who want Murphy caught by any means, including killing him as I got a call from the Waterbury animal control officer telling me the time has come to get him no matter how. He told me the ASPCA or HSUS is going to charge me with animal cruelty. We are trying everything we can, short of lethal means. I contacted him when Murphy was first in Waterbury center and was told he did not catch dogs unless they are a threat or causing trouble. Today he said I did not*

*want his help back then, which is not true. I
am at a loss as to what to do. Many thanks
to all who have helped and supported
our efforts.*

When I read Ed's post, I thought he must've been
exaggerating. I didn't see how anyone could accuse
someone who had been working as hard as Ed to
catch his lost dog with animal abuse. But the next
day I got the same call. I believe the animal control
officer felt strongly that Murphy must've been suf-
fering. Of course I cried when Travis put down Old
Yeller in the 1957 Disney movie about the boy and
his dog who caught rabies after protecting the family from a wolf—but I understood why he pulled the
trigger. However, Murphy was not Old Yeller. He was
a healthy dog, separated from his humans.

Within an hour, I was on the phone with Chris
Nordle, chairman of the Waterbury Select Board,
the head of our local government. Chairman Nordle
didn't take much convincing about the potential
consequences to our town's reputation—with its
growing number of boutique restaurants and craft
beers—should this beautiful lost dog be terminated
by the local authorities. I don't know what happened
behind the scenes in town government, but after
that we never heard anything else from Peter.

7

Emptiness

February 2015

♣ ♣ ♣

We replaced batteries. We set up new cameras. We adjusted our efforts. Peggy, the wolf-tracking expert, advised us that while cats are attracted to dangling bait, canines are often not. Eroc Halperin, the fur trapper, had brought a second game camera, this one set to video, anticipating the capture that never came. Our obsession was almost free-form, unbounded by time. Once inside, when I felt I had nothing more pressing to do, I would study the video. It was better than the still photos at showing how Murphy was acting around the trap.

First he ate the tiny bit of food at the gate. Then he looked at the trap, took a half a step in, and grabbed more bait before darting backward, ever suspicious. He saw the main prize, the big cache of food at the far end of the trap, but he never went for it. He often stood outside the trap, looking into the distance at my house, as though wondering if it was safe to go all the way in.

He's watching us, I thought.

Then he backed out and walked away.

✦ ✦ ✦

The first night the video camera was on, I set the trap, and every few minutes I would go to my back door and shine the spotlight. Usually the trap was empty, the gate up. But when I ran out that night, I saw the food was gone, the gate was closed, and the trap was empty.

He had clearly been in the trap. I was mystified about how he got out. I grabbed the camera's memory card and took it inside.

The video camera records motion in thirty-second increments, then takes a few seconds to reset. Together, the first few sequences of video and images from the still cameras solved the mystery: Murphy was trapped, then escaped. It seems that he didn't immediately realize he had been caught — the video showed him casually eating. But then he started sniffing and pawing at the edges of the trap. He sat quietly for a few minutes, then slowly paced with his tail wagging, the only sign of anxiety his heavy panting in the single-digit temperatures. Once he began to gnaw on the wire enclosure, it didn't take long for Murphy to stick his head through and start to push. The camera reset, so we didn't get to see his escape, but it didn't matter. He was in the trap for twenty-one minutes. And then he wasn't.

I was despondent. How could that dog have known to gnaw his way through the heavy wire and then gotten out so fast? Thankfully, there was no blood in the snow, so, incredibly, chewing on the wire didn't hurt him. Murphy had conquered the contraption that he somehow knew was out to get him. Discouraged beyond belief, I added more food and went back inside. I couldn't set the trap again, of course, until the wire had been strengthened. All I could do was go to sleep and wake up to watch more video in frustration, video that showed him coming back three times that night, going all the way into the trap each time. I almost felt he was taunting me, and I despaired ever getting him into that trap again.

Ed's response the next morning summed it up for all of us:

> *That sucks big time I am at a loss as what to do maybe keep feeding him in to see if he will come back.*

✦ ✦ ✦

Ed, Eroc, and I started discussing what we considered to be our nuclear option: catching Murphy in a fur trapper's leg-hold trap. I confess, we deliberately kept everyone else in the dark about this plan. The downside was obvious. None of us wanted to inflict pain on Murphy, possibly breaking his leg, nor did we wish to further terrify him with human machines, however simple. But Eroc insisted that the traps rarely, if ever, actually broke the bones of the animals he trapped. And the frustration, especially for Ed, had grown too heavy to bear. His doubts, you might say, dogged him.

Eroc works most nights as a bouncer in a Stowe-area bar, so we had to set the trap on a Sunday. Just before dark, a few weeks after Murphy's final escape, Eroc brought three leg-hold traps he used to catch coyotes and buried them in the snow in front of the main trap, now with the hole repaired and the gate open. In the process of setting the traps, he accidentally caught his fingers — it hurt, but didn't break them, a good sign. He also brought night-vision goggles and a thermal-imaging scope so we could watch for Murphy from inside my house and be there within minutes of his capture. Just after dark, we settled in, taking turns watching the trap with the scope. About 9:45 p.m., with Eroc on the scope, Murphy arrived, right on schedule.

"There he is. It's Murphy," Eroc said, his voice rising in expectation as he watched the gray shape come up out of the frozen brook and cross the field.

We all starting yelling and running around my pitch-black kitchen like newbie hunters with their first case of buck fever. We anticipated that Eroc would soon give the word that we had caught him. But Murphy surprised us yet again. While Ed and I ran around the house and Eroc watched, Murphy came toward my home, walked through the back-yard just a few feet from the back door, and then disappeared through the horse pasture into the night. We ran out to check the traps. Somehow Murphy got the food and completely avoided the traps, which remained set. Did he know something was up? Dogs have incredible hearing — had he heard our excitement from inside the house as he walked by?

It was two weeks before the three of us could get together on another Sunday night. This time Eroc brought eight traps. We settled into our vigil without making a peep. Once again, Eroc was on the scope when glowing Murphy arrived, right on schedule, around 10:00 p.m.

"He's dancing, he's dancing!" Eroc yelled, a sign Murphy was caught in the trap and struggling to escape.

I yelled upstairs to my wife, Kim: "We got him!"

We sent Ed out so he'd be the first to approach, hoping Murphy would relent when he saw the familiar face and heard the reassuring voice of the person who raised him from a pup and was there to free him from the pain of the trap.

But amazingly, the traps were empty. We were mystified, because a few had sprung shut. How in the world did this dog manage to avoid so many traps? A tremendous feeling of dread settled into my stomach. I feared he'd been caught by one of the traps and pulled it with him. I had visions of Murphy hobbling through the woods, the trap attached to his leg, dooming him to infection and death. But all the traps were there. Eroc, who had been sure that a leg-hold trap could catch Murphy in a week, was more puzzled than any of us. I did what I always did. I put more food into the trap and set the gate open so he could eat. Everyone went home, and I went to bed.

Three hours later, just before sunrise, the camera showed Murphy back at the scene, eating the food I'd left him.

8

Entrapment

March 2015

✤ ✤ ✤

We added an electronic alarm, originally designed for ice anglers. We fixed a small transmitter to the trap that had a pin attached to the gate with a string. If it worked the way we expected, the gate would fall, pull the pin, turn on a small red light, and send a signal to what was essentially a 1970s-era pager that would beep, alerting us that the trap had been tripped. Unfortunately, the alarm didn't have the range to penetrate the walls of my house, 250 feet from the trap, but the red light was clearly visible from inside. The system went through a set of four AA batteries almost every day. New ones kept appearing in my mudroom.

Erika contributed a small electromagnetic trigger that screwed to the inside of the trap and brought our trapdoor into the twenty-first century.

When a laser beam was broken, the magnet would release the gate. While the wiring was complicated, and the new trap mechanism could be hard to set, Murphy could trip it just by walking in. We set the beam for this Rube Goldberg–type contraption about three-quarters of the way into the trap, far enough so that when Murphy broke the beam, the gate would fall without hitting him. And the beeper would again glow red, alerting us inside the house.

Into March, with the warmer weather coming, the brook in my backyard was soon going to open, and if the spring runoff was significant, it could be too deep and fast for Murphy — and me — to cross. So Erika made another trap for my backyard. This one had six panels, each six feet high, assembled into a hexagonal enclosure. She found instructions for a gate that would fall when the trap was tripped. We were able to put it close enough to the house that we could mount another motion-activated video camera, this one connected to the home Wi-Fi signal, that would broadcast live and send an alert when it was triggered.

As long as the water stayed low enough for me to cross, I kept putting food in the trap across the brook, but I never set it. Now I added food to the backyard trap, too. I could predict that Murphy would visit the field trap, then come into my yard and visit the horses. It didn't take long for Murphy to discover the second source of food at the new trap. Erika set the camera to send alerts to both of our phones. On more than one occasion, I was sitting in my living room watching Murphy live on video just a few feet away in my backyard, circling the trap. Only once did we see him put all four feet inside it. And he never tripped it.

I felt numb. We had to keep it up, continue being patient, but patience wasn't getting us anything besides frustration. I never considered quitting. How could I? I had too much invested. But I had no idea how we were going to solve this riddle, especially heading into spring and then summer. Although I wasn't ready to admit it, even to myself, somewhere in the back of my mind I was beginning to realize that if we were going to bring Murphy home alive it wouldn't happen until the following winter, when he was again hungry and desperate for food. But that didn't mean I'd stop feeding him through the warm weather, hoping for a miracle.

The camera continued to record Murphy's visits, which became less frequent. Sometimes he'd go three or four days without showing up. For a time, I'd be as likely to find images of a fox, a skunk, or even field mice as I would Murph — true wildlife was beginning to discover that there was food in the field. One night in late March, a fox cleaned out the trap about an hour before Murphy arrived.

On the nights he didn't show, I always worried that he was dead. And I was always relieved when I'd see him again. When he did show up, he would stare into the trap: still wary, still looking more or less healthy. In thousands of photos from the trail cameras, the only thing that ever looked amiss was a split in Murphy's bushy tail. It was obvious he wasn't finding shelter anywhere because whenever it rained, he was soaked.

✦ ✦ ✦

Murphy, in essence, had become a stray dog. While people kept asking for Murphy updates on Facebook, and TV news crews now and then asked Ed for interviews, we decided we had to dial back the publicity — it was becoming counterproductive. Once, during the winter, we heard how two men, sure they could be the ones to catch Murphy, spotted him during the day in the trailer park. They chased him for two miles up Perry Hill before they finally gave up. Murphy stayed away for three days. The last humiliation, it seemed, came when a construction worker called in a tip: Murphy was basking in the spring sun at the hotel construction site on Blush Hill, about two miles south of my house. Ed was dubious. But by the time he arrived, there was Murphy, not ten feet away. Though unconcerned by the presence of the construction workers, who weren't bothering him, when Ed took a step outside his truck and slammed the door, Murphy bolted.

9

Catching Murphy

June 2015

❖ ❖ ❖

Late spring and the approach of summer meant the return of thick foliage, and Murphy sightings from the people of Waterbury slowed to almost nothing, though he still occasionally appeared in my yard, and the camera continued to capture his image. Without his winter coat, Murphy looked much skinnier.

In mid-June, Kim and I went to Australia to visit our daughter, Lucy, who had been studying there for the second semester of her third year in college, and I gave Ed the run of our property while we were away. He continued to scheme. At first he made a homemade net gun powered by compressed air, but he couldn't get the net to spread out. Then he tracked down a professional net gun that would, he hoped, entangle Murphy for long enough that he could run up to him and attach a leash. The challenge was he had to be close to Murphy, no more than twenty feet or so away, as he had been at the construction site. We had an old canoe in our field that was used as a horse jump, and before I left for Australia, we dragged it closer to the trap, thinking it would be a good blind for Ed to use in his role as a dog sniper.

While I was gone, Ed lay there on a yoga mat, fighting off mosquitoes, waiting for Murphy.

✤ ✤ ✤

One night, after hours under the canoe, Ed was asleep when Murphy showed up. He woke to Murphy's quiet footfalls in the field. He was close enough, and Ed fired the net gun the best he could. To his dismay, the net didn't spread out like it was supposed to, but instead bunched up and hit Murphy on his back. Murphy casually looked over his shoulder at the balled netting on the ground and ignored it, eating the food as if nothing had happened. Then he trotted off into the darkness.

Ed called out, "Murph! Murphy, boy, it's me!"

I returned midsummer to a deeper depression among us than I had left. If we were never going to recover Kirstin's missing dog, what did we suppose we were doing? Worse, the few sightings we'd logged that summer seemed to suggest that Murphy was taunting us and taking risks:

> *He just ran across rte 100 in front of my*
> *truck! It's 9/16 at 4:45. We were next to the*
> *little Bourne's station, down the road from*

the annex but before B and J. Risky business
crossing 2 lanes of traffic during rush hour
but he made it!

— K. Lora, Front Porch Forum

Once it froze outside, ushering in Murphy's second winter, I finally summoned a new idea. I put his food in a stainless-steel bowl, hoping while he licked it, the bowl would slide along the plywood bottom of the icy trap like a hockey puck, leading him far enough inside to trip the beam of the electric eye and trigger the trap. It was all I had left in terms of innovation, and it didn't count for much: most mornings I found the bowl outside the trap, empty. In some photos, you could see him pick up the bowl and carry it a safe distance away to eat in peace.

Murphy knew the routine. He knew my scent and that I intended to feed him. He knew the scent of my dogs, Gilly and Mabel, regular visitors to the trap. He accepted us. But if anyone or anything interrupted the routine, he'd notice. And it would be days before he'd relax again.

By Christmastime, Murphy was again a regular visitor. He'd been eating out of the trap for almost a year. It had caught him once, but it seemed he believed that, finally, the trap meant food, not danger. I would only set the trap on weekend evenings when I was home and could make sure the complicated setup was working properly. Around dark, when our dogs were in for the night and I went out to feed the horses, I'd set the trap, then email Ed and Erika so they'd know and be ready for the call to come get him. Just before bedtime, I'd go out, put the pin under the gate, and disconnect the electric eye to save battery. When I disconnected it, I'd send a follow-up message to stand down: Murphy was free for another night, and we could all go to bed. It could sometimes feel like he was tending to us, setting our schedule, granting us leave, and not the other way around.

✤ ✤ ✤

I almost didn't set the trap the night we finally caught Murphy. Lucy was coming home from a short trip, and Kim and I headed to the airport to pick her up. It was close to 9:00 p.m. before I had a chance to get out to bait and set the trap, with only two or three hours before I would need to turn in for the night. But everything was working, Murphy was around and hungry, and I ultimately decided it was worth the effort.

Once set, I started my usual routine of looking out the back door every few minutes, hoping I'd see the red light from the alarm, but never really expecting it to happen. I stayed up watching a football game while the rest of the house went to bed. When the game finally ended, I gave the trap one last glance, prepared to find it empty again before going out and disconnecting it.

The red light was on.

I nervously picked up Erika's spotlight, opened the back door, and shone it on the trap. The light reflected the red eyes of Murphy, darting back and forth. I quickly grabbed my phone, put on my coat, pulled on my boots, and headed to the field. The fear that Murphy could once again escape me didn't disappear until I came around the corner of my house and saw for sure that he was still there. I didn't want to give him any time to figure out another way to escape. I called and woke up Kim, then Ed, as I made my way toward the field, still dreading that he would slip away and I'd have to call everyone back to tell them Murphy had escaped again. I held my breath as I went down into the open, shallow brook and up into the field, approaching the dog I'd been watching for more than a year. As I neared the trap, Murphy backed into a corner and might have growled at me — I wasn't sure — but it didn't last. I kneeled and stuck my hand inside the wire. He slowly came toward me and sniffed my fingers. I scratched his ears, the first human contact Murphy had in a year and a half. I tried to be calm. Careful. "It's gonna be OK, boy. You're going home," I said. He started licking my fingers. I was elated.

I called Ed again. "I'm petting him," I told him. Then I called Lisa Lovelette, who had done so much and who, it turned out, had been the one supplying the batteries — she had to be there to help reunite Murphy with his family. And Erika, our high-tech accomplice, who we were relying on to secure Murphy outside the trap.

"We got 'im!" I exclaimed.

While waiting for everyone to arrive, I used three of Erika's big panels to make an enclosure so we could open the trap without worrying that Murphy could rush right by us, back into the woods.

Lisa arrived first. Erika made the half-hour trip from Middlesex. And eventually we saw the lights of Ed's truck coming down the road, rumbling steadily to a stop in my driveway. Ed and Pat both got out of the pick-up, and together we crossed the field, waded the brook, and brought them to their dog.

Once Erika was ready, I carefully pulled up the gate. Murphy came out and climbed into her lap and let her slip on a body harness and a regular collar and leash. I waited for him to try to run when he stepped out of the space I'd set up in front of the trap, but he didn't. Erika held the leash to the harness while I held the leash around his neck. I was still prepared to wrestle him to keep him from getting away, but he walked calmly to my house, including wading through the cold water of the brook. We brought him into my garage and shut the door, unplugging the electric door opener so it wouldn't open accidentally if someone leaned against it, giving Murphy another shot at freedom. It was then that the last vestiges of Murphy's wildness melted. Erika recalls the instant Murphy recognized Ed and rolled on his back so Ed, and then the rest of us, could scratch his belly.

After a few minutes Ed and I walked Murphy to Ed's truck. The finality of the situation was somehow beyond us. Everything seemed rote and scripted. It was over. When Ed opened the door, Murphy jumped into the front seat like it was something he had been doing every day for years.

I was too keyed up to sleep. I put the memory card into my computer and watched the Murphy saga conclude. The last image of the on-the-run Murphy showed him darting around the trap, like he had done dozens of times, if not hundreds, in the year he had visited my field. But this time everything, finally, worked just as we'd imagined: Murphy was just hungry enough to go just far enough to trigger the laser. At 10:49 p.m. on Saturday, January 9, 2016, Murphy was caught. I knew people all over the country were still transfixed by Murphy's story. So before I finally went to bed, I posted to Facebook:

559 days after Murphy was last touched by human hands he went home tonight with his owners, thrilled to be among people once again.

Photo Gallery:

The Homecoming

✣ ✣ ✣

Murphy calmly waits in the trap after 559 days on the run, January 10, 2016.

Wilson Ring scratching Murphy's ear while waiting to release him, January 10, 2016.

The team brings Murphy in from the cold to Wilson Ring's garage, January 10, 2016.

Owner Ed Hamel pets Murphy after bringing him in from the outdoors, January 10, 2016.

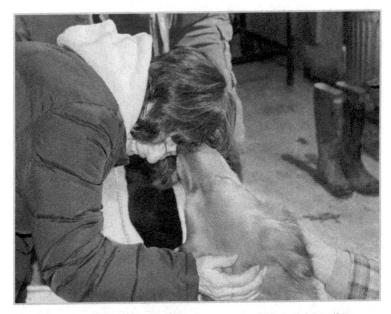

Murphy licks the forehead of owner Pat Hamel in Wilson Ring's garage, January 10, 2016.

Murphy rests before he's brought home by the Hamels, January 10, 2016.

Epilogue

✤ ✤ ✤

Word spread on the internet and onward to the media establishment. Ed, who had been turning down requests for interviews for some time, happily shared the good news with a local TV crew. Later that week, The Boston Globe sent a reporter and photographer to cover the story. In addition to the TV spots, I did interviews on Vermont Public Radio and on the National Public Radio show Here & Now.

Ed used the donations from the fund Lisa had set up to take Murphy for a vet check. He'd been exposed to Lyme disease, but he hadn't gotten sick. The split in his tail was a burdock that was quickly combed out by a local dog groomer who donated a full spa treatment. The shy golden retriever was now a celebrity.

Catching Murphy turned out to be one of the most satisfying things I've ever been involved in. If I'd been told the first time I spotted him that thirteen months would pass before we'd catch him, I honestly don't know what I would have done. People ask me why I did it. I simply answer, "How could I not?" Once I'd started, I couldn't stop.

But the effort took much more than just Ed and me. We couldn't have done it without everyone in Waterbury who reported his movements, donated to his fund, or just kept our spirits up by continuing to care about the animal that was lost among them.

Murphy, Ed, and Pat still live in the Cadys Falls neighborhood of Morrisville, and Kirstin is in a new apartment in Stowe. Ed takes Murphy nearly everywhere he goes, and he stays with Kirstin on the days she doesn't work — good days for reacquainting with an old friend.

Kirstin says she sees a change in Murphy from before he went missing. He's more skittish than ever around people he doesn't know, and he never strays far from his family.

For a long time, they didn't let Murphy off a leash. Now they do.

And he's never made any effort to get away.

Afterword

✤ ✤ ✤

Journalists tell the story, they don't usually become part of the story. My colleague Wilson Ring became part of the story when community members in a Vermont town banded together to try to find a missing golden retriever.

Murphy had been spooked when its owner got into a car accident with the animal in the car in late June of 2014 in Stowe, Vermont. The dog ran off, traumatized. The beloved pet was spotted numerous times in the ensuing months in backyards and on trail cameras in Waterbury Center, where Wilson lives. Whenever someone got close to Murphy, the 3-year-old animal would dart off.

Recognizing Murphy as news but unable to tell the story himself, Wilson asked me to look into it. I spoke with owner Ed Hamel, his granddaughter Kirstin Campbell and I heard their efforts to attract Murphy with rotisserie chicken, bacon, dog toys, and even a psychic that were not enough to catch him.

For more than a year, my co-worker, an animal lover, who owned horses and two dogs regaled me with stories of spotting Murphy on his land that fall. He talked nearly every day of working with Ed to lure Murphy into the trap, all the time worrying about the animal in the cold. Murphy was, however, smarter than the humans who were pursuing him. Once when he was caught, he chewed his way out of the trap, ensuring he stayed free through the summer.

That spring and summer, Murphy wasn't spotted as regularly but Wilson continued to set out food and look for him. The following winter, however, he started to return to Wilson's land more often for food. The group also installed electronics so Wilson could try to monitor any action in the trap from his house. And then one night Murphy was caught in the trap just before 11 p.m. on Jan. 9, 2016, a year and a half after he had run off.

"He was happy to see me, I am very happy to say," Wilson said. That night the dog was reunited with Hamel and his wife and licked their faces. The group, including Murphy, got together for a reunion this summer.

— Lisa Rathke, AP Reporter, Vt.

Bonus Section

♣ ♣ ♣

A "Catching Murphy" Reunion

Left to Right: Eroc Halperin, Lucy Ring, Wilson Ring, Pat Hamel, Ed Hamel and Kirsten Campbell.

In August 2018 I had a reunion with some of the "Murphy" crew to celebrate the upcoming publication of "Catching Murphy."

Murphy, now a little grey in the face as he hits canine middle age, was of course the star of the evening. There is also some fat on his ribs, but after a few minutes the normally shy dog was leaning up against me as though I was a member of his family. I'd like to think he recognized my voice, my smell and perhaps my face, as the one who kept feeding him through the bitterest Vermont winter in years. Even when that brutal winter passed and he didn't need the food from the trap any longer, he continued to visit my field just to see what was there waiting for him.

During our reunion at a Morrisville barbecue restaurant I asked the members of our gang a few questions so they could look back and reflect.

— Wilson Ring, Waterbury, Vt., 2018

✦ ✦ ✦

Ed Hamel, Owner

Wilson Ring: Ed, what did you learn most from your involvement in this experience?

Ed Hamel: It tells me you've got to persevere and keep on going. It was well worth it. I'm glad we got him back.

WR: What would you have felt if someone would have told you it would take 559 days to get him back?

EH: I'd have told them they were crazy. I figured we'd have him in a week. Of course, I thought he'd come back to us too. Little did we know he wouldn't. And that was the whole problem of the whole thing. He didn't want to come back, he wanted to, but didn't dare, I guess. The psychic said he didn't like his name. He wanted to change his name or he wasn't going to come home, or something like that. It was very strange.

✦ ✦ ✦

Pat Hamel, Owner

WR: Pat, you had to endure this whole saga too — What was that like?

PH: I used to tell Ed, remember, 'you've got to be smarter than what you're trying to catch.' It was fun standing by the side of the road with squeak toys, sitting up in the Christmas tree farm, waiting for somebody that never showed up. It's great to have him back, back to his normal self, although what's normal? As I always say, what's normal for one is not necessarily what's normal for someone else.

WR: So, what's the message or take-away for people after reading "Catching Murphy?"

PH: Don't give up. You've got to be persistent.

✦ ✦ ✦

Kirstin Campbell, Ed & Pat's Granddaughter

WR: And how about you Kirstin? Do you agree with your grandparents?

KC: Yes. I'm just really glad to have him home. It was really surprising to see the community come in and help us get him back. I thought it was going to be just us trying to find him, going out and trailing the woods, we actually got dozens of people to help us. That was really inspiring to me, just all the people that, you know, related.

WR: And your message to those who read or listen to this story?

KC: My message would be just keep trying, keep going, anything worth anything is going to take some time and hard work to get at.

✤ ✤ ✤

Eroc Halperin, Wilderness Expert & Trapper

WR: Eroc, you thought catching Murphy would be done in no time, right?

EH: Yes. I still can't believe, when I came on, that it took longer than a couple of weeks, especially with my background. Even though he did eat his way out in the first two weeks, he was one of the toughest animals I've ever had to match wits with and helping Ed change the trap configuration, taking the pressure plate off, finally paid off in the end.

WR: And having gone through all that, what's your message to the world?

EH: My message to the world? Dogs are definitely smarter than people.

✦ ✦ ✦

Lucy Ring, Wilson's Daughter

WR: So Lucy, was there anything that surprised you during the search for Murph?

LR: I was really surprised by, like Kirstin said, the community that came around it. I mostly saw it from Facebook and from talking to you, Dad. I never actually saw him until the night we caught him.

WR: And as someone who joined the effort at a later point, what's stayed with you the most?

LR: The support, just asking, pushing people to have him found, really kept us going.

AP Reports

Bacon, pet psychic turn up zilch in search for dog

By Lisa Rathke

12/10/2014 04:01:43 PM EST

MONTPELIER, Vt. (AP)—Rotisserie chicken, bacon, dog toys, more than a dozen volunteers and even a psychic have not been enough to find Murphy, an elusive golden retriever whose owner's five-month search for the beloved animal has captivated one mountainous area of Vermont.

Neighbors have pulled together to try to find Murphy since he was spooked by a car accident and ran off June 29, going door-to-door with posters, looking for tracks and setting out food and traps.

He's been spotted numerous times, in backyards and on trail cameras in Waterbury Center, about 8 miles from the crash. But any time someone gets close, the 3-year-old cagey canine darts off.

"I definitely think he's still in the fight-or-flight mode because he seems to run from everybody," said his owner, 24-year-old Kirstin Campbell, of Morrisville.

Campbell had Murphy with her when her vehicle went off the road and hit a tree in Stowe. She let the dog out after the crash and he ran away, traumatized. He was seen around the resort town in the summer but ended up venturing south to Waterbury Center, apparently along the one main road between the towns.

The search has gotten the attention of local media and members of a popular online community forum where Campbell's grandfather Ed Hamel, 63, has posted weekly since Murphy disappeared.

"We did the old, you know, put the clothing out, put the towels out, food out, treats out, walk around and walk around, leave our scent everywhere and that didn't do any good," said Hamel, who describes Murphy as "the best dog in the world."

At one point they enlisted a Massachusetts-based pet psychic who claims to be able to communicate with animals. The psychic told them by phone that Murphy was on a parallel path to a road where they had just lost track of him and that she was seeing his name. A tipster then reported seeing Murphy at Murray Hill Farm in Waterbury Center, Campbell said.

After Murphy was spotted in August, one woman drove about 30 miles from Burlington every night to keep a look out for him in Waterbury Center.

And town resident Lisa Lovelette has helped check the traps for Hamel, knowing he couldn't come twice a day.

"I just thought about how I would feel if it were

my dog and I lived 30 miles away," she said. "So I've just been doing what I can to kind of help him out."

At the end of October and in mid-November, Murphy was spotted on two trail cameras in Waterbury Center, giving Campbell hope that he's still out there and they're on the right track.

Now one homeowner nearby has been setting out food to lure Murphy back for regular feedings until he can be caught — before winter really sets in.

But Hamel and Campbell urged people not to chase the skittish pooch, just to report where they see him.

"I miss him like crazy," she said.

Photo Gallery:

The Trail Cam

✤ ✤ ✤

8   0°F ◐ 0 2 / 0 2 / 2 0 1 5 0 5 : 0 6 PM BAMERA 1

Murphy stares at the trail camera at dusk after looking for food in the trap, February 2, 2015.

░-31°F (02/16/2015 11:11PM BAMERA1

Temperatures below -20 degrees were common, but the -31 shown on the trail camera was the coldest night recorded. Murphy needed the food left for him, February 16, 2015.

5°F) 03/24/2015 10:21PM BAMERA1

Other animals discovered the food left in the trap, like this hungry fox, March 24, 2015.

Murphy resting comfortably next to the trap while digesting his latest meal, April 1, 2015.

It was easier to tell how much weight Murphy lost after shedding his winter coat, July 22, 2015.

Wilson Ring's daughter Lucy (right) and wife Kim Parsons talk to Murphy after he was finally caught, January 10, 2016.

About the Author

Photo © Lisa Rathke

Wilson Ring is the Vermont correspondent for the Associated Press. A native Vermonter, Ring served in the Peace Corps in Ecuador and worked as a free-lance reporter in Central America before returning to Vermont. He is a recipient of The Associated Press Media Editors Charles Rowe award.

Acknowledgments

✤ ✤ ✤

Keeping Murphy, the scared golden retriever, healthy and alive for more than a year in my Vermont neighborhood was truly a community effort. While I was feeding him daily and checking the trail camera that marked his frequent visits to my horse pasture, most everyone in town was watching out for him. Murphy would probably be dead were it not for the people of Waterbury and Stowe who reported their Murphy sightings nearly every day from shortly after he escaped until just before we caught him, on the online bulletin board Front Porch Forum or Facebook. The reports gave those of us on the Murphy crew regular updates of his movements, even if they scared us because we knew how often the dog that had never been around a road was regularly crossing — probably several times a day — Vermont Route 100, the state's main north-south highway that follows the spine of the Green Mountains from Massachusetts to the Canadian border.

Meeting Ed Hamel and his family and getting to know them was a privilege I cherish. Ed's unwavering commitment to resolving the mystery of the lost family dog blew me away. He never forgot his responsibility as a dog owner and, as stressful as the search was, he never let up. When I told him my barn boots were getting wet crossing the brook to check the trap or the camera, a pair of waders appeared in my garage. He provided the trail camera that tracked Murphy's movements for more than a year. Whenever food would get low, it would appear. The best phone call I ever made in my life came around midnight on Jan. 9, 2016 when I woke him up to tell him Murphy was safely in the trap.

Lisa Lovelette, the retired school principal, made sure everyone in Waterbury was watching for Murphy. She set up the account that allowed people to donate to the Murphy fund and was always ready to help when needed.

Erika Holm, the animal control officer in the neighboring town of Middlesex, brought her years-long experience in catching lost dogs into the search. And when the triggers we were using in the trap kept failing, she kept supplying ever-more expensive pieces of electronic equipment that, ultimately, caught him. Erika also brought to the Murphy search a number of her animal-loving friends, all of whom supplied everything from their ideas to high-end dog food.

Peggy Strushacker, the wolf-tracking expert who used her tracking prowess to learn about Murphy's movements in the neighborhood, provided a huge hunk of past-its-sell-date prime rib donated by a Stowe supermarket that kept Murphy alive during a January stretch when the air temperatures were around minus-thirty.

Eroc Halperin, the coyote trapper, who Ed brought to the search and famously said he saw no reason we couldn't catch Murphy in a week. (In a sense he was right. Murphy was caught right on Eroc's schedule, but he didn't calculate that Murphy would chew his way out of the trap, all of which was caught on the second trail camera Eroc provided that we set to video.) He helped with the mechanics of the running the trap. He also never gave up and was an enthusiastic member of the Murphy crew right up until the night we caught him.

I'd also thank former AP East Editor Karen Testa, who right around the time we caught Murphy sent a memo asking reporters with ideas for a book to get in touch with Peter Costanzo, AP's Digital Publishing Specialist and Mimi Polk Gitlin, AP's Head of Media Development and Production in Los Angeles, both of whom helped adjust my lifetime of wire-service writing into the story of Murphy and his 559 days on the run in the wilds of Vermont.